VR ON THE JOB
Understanding Virtual and Augmented Reality

USING VR IN MEDICINE

Cathleen Small

Cavendish Square

New York

Published in 2020 by Cavendish Square Publishing, LLC
243 5th Avenue, Suite 136, New York, NY 10016

Library of Congress Cataloging-in-Publication Data

Names: Small, Cathleen, author.
Title: Using VR in medicine / Cathleen Small.
Other titles: Using virtual reality in medicine
Description: First edition. | New York : Cavendish Square Publishing, 2020. |
Series: VR on the job: understanding virtual and augmented reality |
Audience: Grades 7 to 12. | Includes bibliographical references and index.
Identifiers: LCCN 2019000919 (print) | LCCN 2019003089 (ebook) |
ISBN 9781502645715 (ebook) | ISBN 9781502645708 (library bound) | ISBN 9781502645692 (pbk.)
Subjects: LCSH: Virtual reality in medicine--Juvenile literature. |
Medical innovations--Juvenile literature. | Medicine--Information
technology--Juvenile literature. | Virtual reality--Vocational guidance--Juvenile literature.
Classification: LCC R859.7.C67 (ebook) | LCC R859.7.C67 S63 2020 (print) | DDC 610.285--dc23
LC record available at https://lccn.loc.gov/2019000919

Editorial Director: David McNamara
Editor: Chet'la Sebree
Copy Editor: Nathan Heidelberger
Associate Art Director: Alan Sliwinski
Designer: Christina Shults
Production Coordinator: Karol Szymczuk
Photo Research: J8 Media

The photographs in this book are used by permission and through the courtesy of: Cover Gorodenkoff/Shutterstock.com, background (and used throughout the book) Click Bestsellers/Shutterstock.com; p. 4 Hasloo/iStockphoto.com; p. 7 ImageFlow/Shutterstock. com; p. 10-11 Zapp2Photo/Shutterstock.com; p. 12 Minecraftpsyco/Wikimedia Commons/ File:Sensoramamortonheiligvirtualrealityheadset.Jpg; CC BY SA 4.0; p. 15 Chris J. Ratcliffe/ Bloomberg/Getty Images; p. 16 Peterhowell/Getty Images; p. 18 Photographee.eu/Shutterstock. com; p. 21 Supamotion/Shutterstock.com; p. 25 Katarzyna Bialasiewicz/iStockphoto.com; p. 27 Kittisak Jirasittichai/Shutterstock.com; p. 30 Donald Iain Smith/Getty Images; p. 33 RedPixel.P/ Shutterstock.com; p. 34-35 Gorodenkof/Shutterstock.com; p. 40 George Rudy/Shutterstock.com; p. 44 Alex Traksel/Shutterstock.com; p. 48-49 LightField Studios/Shutterstock.com; p. 50 FatCamera/ E+/Getty Images; p. 54 Khoamartin/Shutterstock.com; p. 56 CandyBox Images/Shutterstock.com; p. 21 Zoranm/E+/Getty Images; p. 61 Stellamc/Shutterstock.com; p. 62 Hattanas/Shutterstock. com; p. 65 Priyanka Parashar/Mint/Getty Images; p. 66-67 Qilai Shen/Bloomberg/Getty Images.

Printed in the United States of America

CONTENTS

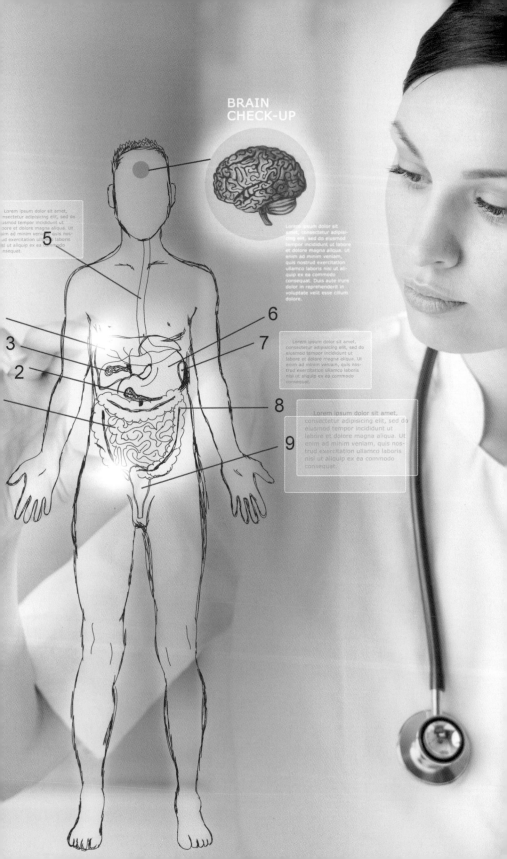

1 THE BASICS

M edicine is an ancient profession. For as long as humans have existed, medicine has existed in some form. For instance, ancient humans used various plants to treat injuries and illnesses, without any of the modern medical knowledge and tools available today. Despite being an old profession, medicine is always changing.

EMERGING TECHNOLOGIES

Over time, new diseases and conditions come into the public consciousness. For instance, there seemingly has been a dramatic increase in autism diagnoses in recent decades. People have also encountered the

Opposite: Virtual and augmented reality can help doctors diagnose patients and develop treatment plans.

painful reality of grave conditions such as acquired immunodeficiency syndrome (AIDS) and Alzheimer's.

As quickly as new diseases and conditions become known, so, too, do new treatments and tools like vaccines become available. For example, the human papillomavirus (HPV) vaccine was first introduced in the early twenty-first century. Treatments for diseases like Alzheimer's are extending lifespans. And targeted chemotherapy is showing much promise for treating certain types of cancer that decades ago carried a much more dire prognosis.

But it's not just medications and treatments that transform medicine. Sometimes it's technology. Virtual reality (VR) and augmented reality (AR) are two relatively new technologies that are helping educate patients and future physicians, preparing surgeons for and guiding them in difficult operations, and even providing virtual assistance during procedures.

Before taking a good look at how VR and AR are transforming the field of medicine, it's important to know the differences between the two technologies.

THE DIFFERENCES

The differences between VR and AR may not be immediately apparent. Most people know that VR and AR involve some sort of simulated reality. However, they may not know exactly what each technology is and how each works.

VR headsets generally incorporate visual and auditory components to help immerse the user in the virtual experience.

The names of the technologies provide good clues. The word "virtual" means "almost, but not quite." For instance, a person might describe two brands of cola as tasting "virtually the same." This means the two sodas taste almost the same, but not quite.

In virtual reality, it's the world or environment that is almost the same as the real world, but not quite. For example, using VR technology, a particular location might look almost the same, but not be exactly the same, as it is a digital recreation of a particular landscape. Software developers have created VR applications for travel that allow a person to visit such places as the Grand Canyon or the Great Wall of China, all from the comfort of their own home. That's because they're visiting a virtual representation of these places.

Augmented reality, on the other hand, does not attempt to virtually re-create a location or experience. The word "augmented" describes something that has been enhanced in some way. Certain plastic surgery procedures, for example, are known as "augmentations." These surgeries involve adding to some part of the body to make it larger or improve upon it. People refer to augmenting their income when they make it greater in some way.

In AR technology, reality is changed by adding something to it. In gaming, for example, *Pokémon Go* is a great example of AR technology in action. The game uses a mobile device's GPS to show a map of the area, but that map is augmented by the addition of various Pokémon that can be "caught" by players. In short, VR generates a representation of an entire reality, whereas AR takes the reality that already exists and simply adds to it.

Another difference between VR and AR is in the equipment used. VR generally requires a headset and sometimes hand controllers or even an exoskeleton, or bodysuit, to allow a user to experience and manipulate the virtual world. Many VR experiences integrate sound to add to the experience. Some even integrate smells. For example, Disney's California Adventure theme park featured an early virtual reality ride called Soarin' Over California. Riders sat in a seat that was meant to mimic a hang-gliding experience and virtually "flew" over the landscape of California. Wind was generated to add to the experience. As riders flew over the orange groves of California, they could breathe in the scent of orange blossoms. The motion of the ride, the feel of the wind, the smell of the orange blossoms, and the realistic video depicted on a giant screen in front of riders made the experience feel very much like a real flight above California. The ride has since been updated and changed its name to Soarin' Around the World.

AR, on the other hand, doesn't always require specialized gear. It does require technology, of course. For *Pokémon Go*, for example, users can play on a smartphone or tablet. But some AR programs do use additional technology, such as smart glasses. These glasses allow the user to see the world as a person would through normal glasses, with the addition of digital elements on the lenses.

VR AND AR IN MEDICINE

Some of the biggest milestones related to virtual reality happened in the mid- to late twentieth century. These milestones largely explored the possibilities of this new technology. Once the possibilities for VR and AR technology became apparent, different fields developed

Augmented reality overlays information on top of an actual representation of a place or item. This AR overlay identifies the different parts under the hood of a car.

specialized applications to use the new technology. The medical field was one of them.

Scientists and researchers began to explore medicine-specific applications for VR and AR in the early 1980s. Research teams at the Department of Defense and at the University of North Carolina started testing VR headsets and their use for simulating medical procedures on computer-generated images. As the technology has advanced, such simulators have even begun to use haptic force feedback to simulate the feeling of performing surgery. Haptic force feedback is a type of physical response in which force, vibration, and movement are used to virtually create the sense of touch.

In the mental health field, VR therapy has been found useful in treating anxiety and depression, as well as social difficulties and attention-deficit hyperactivity disorder (ADHD). As the technology developed, doctors also began to use it as a form of cognitive behavioral therapy (CBT). CBT is a form of therapy in which negative thoughts about the self are challenged in an attempt to alter unwanted behaviors or treat mood disorders. It has long

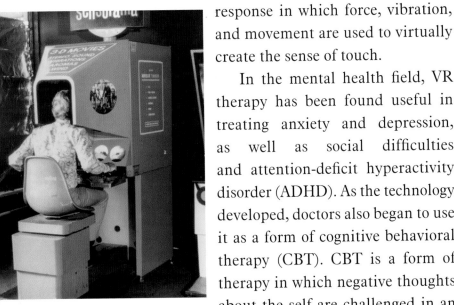

Early VR was developed in the 1960s, even though it didn't make its way into the medical field until the 1980s.

been used as a treatment for certain fears and anxieties. A strategy for treating these conditions is providing a patient with repeated exposure to something that stimulates fear. The plan is that this repeated exposure helps a person eventually overcome the fear. If a person is afraid of riding in a car, for example, the idea behind the therapy is that more instances of safely riding in a car will help the person conquer the worst of their anxiety.

But what if the fear is of something like flying? It is very expensive and not something people do on an everyday basis. In such a case, a virtual-reality experience of flying on a plane could be used to repeatedly expose a patient to the experience of flying without actually requiring daily or weekly plane flights.

More recently, VR has also been used for pain management, stroke and brain damage assessment and rehabilitation, and as a treatment for Alzheimer's disease. Eye conditions that used to require patching can now sometimes be treated with VR treatments, too.

In addition to treatments, these emerging technologies have even helped doctors and medical students. In an educational setting, the Microsoft HoloLens, an AR device, can allow medical professionals and students to practice procedures on holographic models of the human body and its organs. In past years, medical students used cadavers for practice, which has certain limitations. Cadavers are preserved dead bodies that have been donated to science.

Once you've performed a splenectomy on a cadaver, the cadaver no longer has an intact spleen for other students to practice on. Holograms, however, can be regenerated an infinite number of times, which would allow for more opportunities to practice.

Other AR applications in medicine include ProjectDR. This application allows doctors to view overlaid images developed from medical scans on a patient's body.

VR and AR technologies are changing rapidly. However, despite their relatively recent entry into the medical field, they are showing much promise for reshaping how students learn to become doctors, how patients are treated, how surgeries are performed, and how mental-health issues are addressed.

DR. SHAFI AHMED

If patients need colorectal, or colon and rectum-related, surgery in the London area and want to go to the best, they go to Dr. Shafi Ahmed. However, Dr. Ahmed isn't just a gifted surgeon. He is also a technology pioneer. He is the cofounder of Medical Realities, a platform that allows students to learn from skilled surgeons who teach interactive classes using VR technology.

In 2014, Dr. Ahmed was the first doctor to live-stream a surgery using Google Glass, a type of smart glasses. Just two years later, he performed the first operation to be streamed live in 360-degree video. This live stream also provided audiences with the first virtual reality experience of a surgery, using a VR headset and a smartphone. According to an article in the *Telegraph*, "the operation ... [was] filmed on two 360 degree cameras with multiple lenses."

Dr. Shafi Ahmed uses a variety of hardware, like the Microsoft HoloLens headset he is shown wearing here, during his surgeries.

In the VR experience, viewers could "zoom in on Dr. Ahmed's movements and walk around the operating theatre to see the operation from different angles." People in 140 countries experienced the surgery through the wonders of technology. Dr. Ahmed has even used Snapchat Spectacles to share clips of his surgeries.

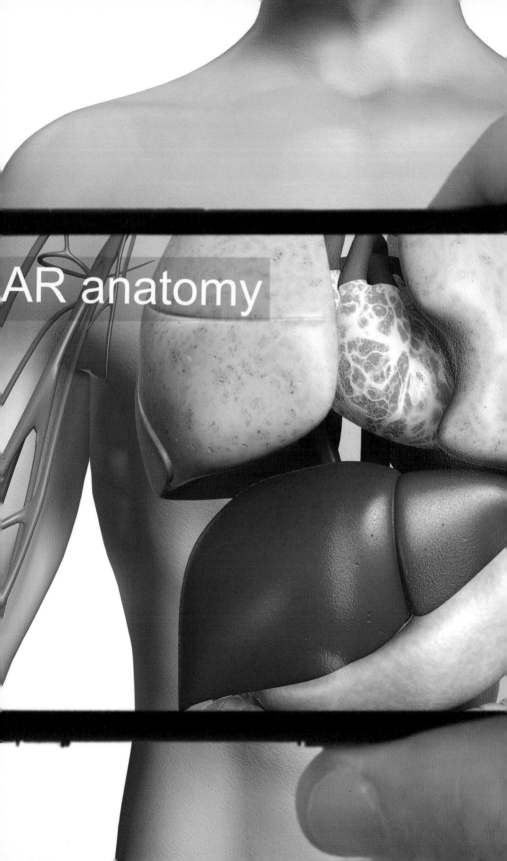

AR anatomy

2 PRACTICAL APPLICATIONS

Since medical professionals began to use VR and AR in the field, the uses have become varied. VR and AR technologies are used in everything from surgery to pain management to the field of mental health. While the technologies certainly help doctors and health-care providers in their work, they also benefit patients in many ways.

VR FOR PAIN MANAGEMENT

One area where patients see a great benefit from VR is in pain management. Historically, pain management has involved drug treatments, such as anti-inflammatory or opioid medications. However, there are long-term risks

Opposite: X-ray vision doesn't exist, but AR can simulate it by showing the user an image of what's inside a body.

Some patients with chronic or acute pain can find relief through VR applications.

associated with these treatments. Other treatments have involved relaxation or mental-health techniques such as hypnosis and biofeedback. The latter technique is a process in which automatic bodily functions, like breathing, are monitored. The information collected is used to train a patient to develop control over those functions, like slowing down his or her breath. In recent years, though, VR has been found effective in pain management and relief for those suffering from short-term and long-term pain.

According to researchers, the pain-relieving effects of VR may be a result of the technology stimulating various affective, or emotion-based, and attention-based body processes that help each person manage their pain. In other words, for some patients pain may be able to be managed by changing a mindset or changing a person's focus. This technology has been used on patients undergoing painful procedures. Although researchers aren't entirely sure how the VR helps patients, the patients have reported less pain and an interest in using the technology again during future procedures.

There are several different pain-management VR applications. One called Karuna uses the technology to help patients retrain their brains to react to painful stimuli. Another called Oncomfort combines various treatments for stress management and anxiety management in a VR experience to reduce pain. The creators built the application off the theory that stress and anxiety increase pain responses.

VR FOR MEMORY FUNCTION

Pain management is just one of the many uses for VR in medicine. Using VR, scientists are learning more about how the brain processes and stores memories. They are hopeful that the information they gain will eventually lead to more targeted therapies and treatments for people facing conditions associated with memory loss like dementia and Alzheimer's disease. Researchers at UCLA, for example, are using VR and implants in patients' brains to detect how their brains form and store memories developed during movement.

AR AND VR IN SURGERY

Surgery is a field of intense precision. However, the human body doesn't always follow the rules. A patient's internal organs may look a little different from what is typical. This presents an added challenge for surgeons. On the flip side, the patient's organs may look very typical. However, the surgery needed may be one that a surgical team hasn't performed before. For these reasons, practice is essential for surgeons.

In the past, surgeons learned through books, by viewing surgeries performed by other surgeons, and by operating on a cadaver. In more recent years, surgeons have also learned by viewing computer-modeled images. For most people, learning by doing is incredibly useful. Virtual reality has made this possible. Some VR technology has allowed surgeons to perform virtual surgeries before actually setting foot in the operating room.

At the University of Basel in Switzerland, for example, surgeons can practice on 3D images in a virtual space. They can perform the surgery in a realistic environment and on realistic organs. This experience is valuable because, according to Dr. Justin Barad, surgeons need

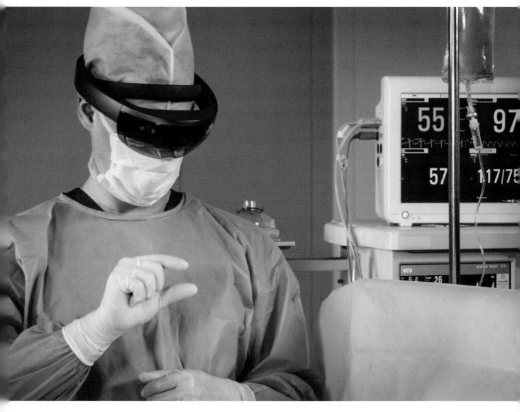

Surgeons can use AR technology to help guide them through intricate surgeries.

to perform a given surgery fifty to one hundred times to do it well. Surgical residents observe many surgeries and typically practice on cadavers before performing a surgery on a patient. Residents are medical school graduates participating in specialized practice under the supervision of a physician. Because their opportunities to perform actual surgeries are limited, they begin their surgical careers without a lot of practical experience. Using

VR to virtually perform surgeries gives surgical residents much-needed training.

Dr. Barad, a pediatric orthopedist, is the CEO and founder of Osso VR. Orthopedics is a branch of medicine associated with muscle and bone. Barad's company provides surgical training and VR experiences specific to orthopedic and spinal surgeries. However, there are other VR applications being used to train surgeons in other surgeries as well.

For example, ImmersiveView uses CT and MRI scan data to create a "digital twin" of a patient. CTs and MRIs are two different technologies that provide doctors with images of patients' bones and internal organs. With ImmersiveView, doctors can use the VR twin created out of these scans to view the target part of the anatomy. However, more than just viewing it, they can also handle the digital body part and turn it in any direction to get a better view. In other words, ImmersiveView brings traditional, static CT and MRI scans to life for each individual patient. If ImmersiveView sounds incredible, the reality is even more amazing. Forty surgeons in India recently used the VR platform to practice for an incredibly delicate and rare surgical procedure. They were practicing separating conjoined twins who were connected at their heads.

Similarly, AR has entered the surgical field. A number of applications have shown great promise. Typically, surgeons have had to look away from their patients to examine scans as they are performing procedures. Using AR, scan data can be overlaid on the patient's body so the surgeon does not have to constantly look away and then look back at the patient. For example, Stryker has developed a TGS (Target Guided Surgery) navigation system for sinus surgeries. It uses AR to map data from a preoperative plan and scans of a person's body taken by a tube with a small camera and light called an endoscope. The technology provides real-time guidance for the procedure. This results in a minimally invasive and highly accurate sinus surgery based on the patient's anatomy. In fact, AR generally could be key in making surgeries less invasive. In theory, AR could allow surgeons to make a much smaller incision than was done in the past, while still "seeing" an accurate picture of the inside of a person's body.

Microsoft's HoloLens, a holographic computer headset, is considered a promising piece of hardware for future AR applications in surgery. It can also use MRI and CT scans to develop sophisticated mapping systems like the one developed by a technology team at Cambridge Consultants. However, surgeons such as Dr. Shafi Ahmed caution that AR applications for surgery still need further development. One of the biggest issues is that the body can move and change a bit between when a scan is taken and when surgery is performed. For that reason, the overlaid data may not be 100 percent accurate when the patient is actually in surgery. The AR applications need to be able to adjust the AR image relative to any subtle changes in anatomy.

VR AND MENTAL HEALTH

Anxiety, phobias, and post-traumatic stress disorder (PTSD) are common mental-health conditions that plague many, many people. For some, anxiety may negatively impact their daily life. However, these individuals may still be able to attend school, hold a job, and raise a family. For others, phobias and PTSD can be crippling disorders that can leave them unable to lead happy lives and participate in society.

Cognitive behavior therapy (CBT) has long been used to treat a variety of mental-health conditions, with anxiety, phobias, and PTSD being among them. One type of CBT is exposure therapy. It can help a person lessen his or her reaction to a stressor. For example, a person with a crippling fear of flying might begin by watching videos of flights. Then, he or she may go on a series of visits to the airport to walk through the process of parking the car and walking into the terminal. They would slowly, through repeated exposure, work up to being able to actually board a plane and take a flight.

VR has been found to be an extremely effective platform for exposure therapy. It provides a strikingly realistic experience. Additionally, it does so in one place. This is much easier for patients than potentially having to go to a separate site (such as an airport) as they work through their phobias. The VR technology also takes away the possibility for unknown environmental changes. Suppose a person with a fear of flying goes to the airport and walks into the

People suffering from PTSD, phobias, or anxiety may be helped by exposure therapy via VR devices and applications.

terminal as part of therapy. However, that particular day the terminal is shut down because of a suspicious package or bomb threat. Imagine the setback that would provide to the patient. With VR, these types of external factors are controllable.

Not only can external factors be controlled, but internal factors can be tracked. In other words, data about a patient's

THE FLIP SIDE

For a patient, VR can be incredibly promising in treating mental-health conditions and managing pain. But there are some safety concerns with VR that must be considered as well. Some users of VR have reported nausea, dizziness, blurred vision, and disorientation. Users who suffer from seizure disorders are at an increased risk for seizure activity when using VR. The use of the technology has also been known to trigger migraines in some users prone to them. People with schizophrenia, a condition in which sufferers are usually withdrawn from reality, are also cautioned against using VR. The realistic, simulated environments can make their delusions worse.

There are a host of these sorts of concerns surrounding VR even for users who are completely healthy. For instance, somewhat ironically, VR can actually trigger PTSD in people if they are exposed to violent or frightening situations that are extremely realistic. Additionally, if a VR application involves any sort of movement, people are at risk of falling or bumping into objects in the real environment. Furthermore, VR has been shown to affect the growth of the eye, especially in children, which can lead to nearsightedness.

As with most things, moderation seems to be key. Most experts agree that VR is safe when used in appropriate circumstances and in moderation.

As with many treatments, VR can have some side effects and should be used in moderation and in consultation with a trained professional.

physical and mental responses can be tracked through this technology. This capability is immensely helpful for therapists treating patients with anxiety, phobias, or PTSD. With these conditions, a patient's body actually changes and reacts to stress. Patients may begin sweating, their heart rate may increase, and their breathing may become fast or shallow. It's important for doctors and therapists to be able to monitor these physical changes so they can tailor the therapy to the patient.

Virtual reality graded exposure therapy (VRGET) handles all of these factors. It uses 3D visual displays and advanced graphics as well as smells, sounds, and physical sensations to make a simulated environment feel just like the environment that causes stress for the patient. As the patient is using the technology, the therapist receives feedback from body-tracking technologies that monitor heart rate, respiration, and other physical data that indicate stress levels in the patient. Therapists can use VRGET with people at risk for developing PTSD and assess the data provided to determine whether a person is likely to develop the condition. In that way, therapists can be proactive with their treatment plan. Similarly, VR has been used for stress-resilience training, in which people at high risk for developing PTSD are taken through stressful situations and guided to develop coping strategies that involve relaxation.

A FUTURE IN THE FIELD

To detail all of the applications of VR and AR in medicine would be nearly impossible, especially since the field is changing by the day. However, it's clear that as VR and AR development continue, and as the field of medicine changes, the potential applications of VR and AR will continue to grow. This will benefit both health-care providers and patients alike. It also means that the job market will continue to expand.

3

VR AND AR JOBS IN MEDICINE

Development of applications using VR and AR technology is progressing quickly, which means there is no shortage of jobs in this exciting field. There are many directions to consider for those interested in working in VR and AR in the medical area. These jobs range from software and hardware development and quality assurance (QA) to careers in psychology specializing in the use of VR as a treatment protocol.

Opposite: Virtual representations of the human body can provide excellent training tools for doctors.

SOFTWARE ENGINEERS

Level:	Varies
Years of Experience Required:	Varies
Education Needed:	Bachelor's degree in computer science or a related field
Skills Needed:	Strong analytical and communication skills, creativity, attention to detail, and strong problem-solving skills

There are jobs in both the VR and AR fields to work on both hardware and software. Hardware includes headsets, hand controllers, and even exoskeletons that users wear during their VR or AR experiences. Software describes the VR and AR programs that run through the hardware. So, for example, a person can own a VR headset. However, without software to run, the headset won't do anything. With a headset, users can download many different software packages for different VR and AR experiences.

In the medical field, the software is likely to be more specialized. Someone using VR for gaming might download many different packages to play with, but a medical practice using VR is more likely to have a specialized software package they use exclusively. For instance, OSSA VR makes software specific to orthopedic and spinal surgeries.

VR and AR hardware components are only as good as the software they are running. This software is often created by a team of engineers.

Either way, though, someone needs to develop the software that's used. That's where the job of software engineer comes in. Software engineers are also sometimes referred to as software developers or programmers. However, in general, they do the same thing. They work (usually on a team) to develop VR and AR programs.

The requirements to become a VR or AR software engineer vary widely, depending on the position. Some jobs do not require previous VR or AR development experience, but some do. Some do not require a college degree, but many do. It just depends on the position, although generally the bigger, better-known companies will have more requirements than newer start-ups. Start-ups often don't pay as much, so they are sometimes more willing to hire a relative newbie to the field. The

Knowledge of 3D art software will help those interested in building VR and AR software. Learning art and design programs, even if just for fun, will help you with a career in developing VR and AR for the medical field.

better-known companies often offer higher pay and more stability. For those reasons, they are able to attract software engineers with more experience.

For example, the Centers for Disease Control and Prevention (CDC), a major national organization, had a job listing for an AR/VR programmer to work on a software development team. The candidate and team would be responsible for storyboarding, prototyping, and creating digital wireframe images, or 3D skeletal models. Storyboarding is the creation of a sequence of drawings that helps designers and engineers plan visuals for the technology. Prototyping involves the creation of an initial model that can be recreated. In this way, the person in this role would be responsible for much of the creation of the idea and the project from start to finish.

For this position, which came with a nearly six-figure salary and a competitive benefits package, applicants were expected to have at least a bachelor's degree in science game art and design or a related field. The CDC also expected candidates to have at least three to five years of experience in developing strong relationships and working collaboratively. Those were the minimum qualifications. However, the CDC preferred applicants to have experience working with the Unity game engine. A game engine is a software development environment on which people build video games. While this particular position had nothing to do with gaming (and everything to do with medicine and medical policy), a lot of VR and AR development is done through the Unity or Unreal game engines.

In general, those interested in a career in VR or AR software development would be wise to learn how to program for Unity or Unreal, even if they don't aspire to a career in game design.

Additionally, people interested in software engineering should have experience in a variety of programming languages. Developers and engineers use the languages to build software. There are many languages, and some are far more commonly used than others. In general, common languages include Python, C# (pronounced "C sharp"), and C. Experience in one of these common languages will make learning other less common languages much easier. Many employers are willing to allow applicants to learn a new language if they're not familiar with it, as long as the applicant has strong experience with some similar programming language.

HARDWARE ENGINEERS

Level:	Mid-level
Years of Experience Required:	Seven to ten years, depending on level of education
Education Needed:	Bachelor's or master's degree in electrical engineering or a related field
Skills Needed:	Experience with electrical engineering, experience working with software developers, proven record of advanced technology product development, and strong collaborative skills

Software is one piece of the VR and AR development picture, and hardware is the other piece. Sometimes AR requires nothing more than a smartphone or tablet, but other times it requires additional equipment. VR always requires equipment such as a headset, hand controllers, sensors, and sometimes exoskeletons.

Even though many of these pieces of equipment already exist, they are constantly being further developed. For example, VR headsets started out being very heavy. Hardware engineers are constantly working on ways to make headsets lighter and more comfortable. Similarly, they are always looking for ways to make hand controllers more responsive and earphones more comfortable and clearer.

While software engineer positions run the range from beginner to advanced developer, hardware engineer positions in VR and AR tend to be relatively advanced positions for highly skilled engineers. For example, Microsoft's HoloLens is a piece of AR hardware that is showing great promise for medical AR applications. A job posting for a senior mechanical engineer on the HoloLens team called for applicants to have at least five years of experience in mechanical product development and at least five years of experience in designing mechanical systems. The job posting also called for a number of highly specialized mechanical engineering and design skills. Another posting for a senior hardware engineer on the HoloLens team called for at least ten years of experience in developing and manufacturing specific technology as well as a master's degree or PhD in mechanical engineering, electrical engineering, or physics. Microsoft is obviously a big-name company, and the HoloLens is a high-profile product. The high-level requirements make sense.

A smaller start-up might relax their required qualifications a bit if they found capable hardware engineers willing to take a chance on a less established company. Regardless, people interested in a career in hardware engineering should plan to earn at least a bachelor's degree, if not a master's or PhD. They should also find entry-level work in a related hardware-engineering field so they can gain enough experience to be a serious candidate for a hardware engineering position in VR and AR.

PSYCHOLOGISTS

Level:	Varies
Years of Experience Required:	Varies
Education Needed:	Master's degree or doctor of psychology (Psy.D.)
Skills Needed:	Strong listening and communication skills, high level of integrity and empathy, patience, and strong problem-solving and interpersonal skills

Those interested in using VR technology to treat patients might enjoy a career in psychology with a specialty in virtual reality exposure therapy.

Not every job in VR and AR in the medical field is a technical one. The technical jobs are for the people who create and refine the hardware and software that make up a VR or AR experience. But what about the people who use the VR and AR products in a medical setting? Those would be doctors and psychologists.

Many different types of doctors can use VR in their work. Surgeons are one example. Ophthalmologists, who diagnose and treat eye disorders, are another. However, their use of VR and AR technologies is likely fairly minimal, unless they have chosen to very narrowly specialize in procedures in which the technologies are commonly used. However, for those interested in helping people on a more regular basis using these types of technologies, psychology can be a good career to pursue.

Like physicians, psychologists likely use VR for some patients but not others. For example, a particular treatment for PTSD called eye movement desensitization and reprocessing (EMDR) is used for some survivors of trauma. Psychologists can earn certifications as an EMDR practitioner, and then they can use the treatment as they see fit. EMDR may make up a very small part of their practice, depending on the patients they see. But if a psychologist feels strongly that EMDR is a type of therapy they can be very effective with, they may choose to specialize their practice and mainly see patients seeking this type of treatment.

For instance, a psychologist can choose to market themselves mainly to clients seeking virtual reality exposure therapy (VRET). Some psychologists become well known for their work with a certain type of treatment. For those interested in VR, creating a specialized practice based on VRET is a viable career option.

This is particularly true for private-practice psychologists, who essentially set their own hours and are their own bosses. Psychologists employed by a hospital, clinic, or government facility (such as the US Department of Veterans Affairs) may have more limits placed on their practice, depending on the expectations of the facility. However, the job outlook is very strong for psychologists. The Bureau of Labor Statistics projected a 14 percent increase in jobs in this field between 2016 and 2026. From that projection, it is reasonable to assume that a skilled psychologist would have little problem setting up a private practice with a specialization like VR.

For those not interested in private practice but still interested in working with VR in their practice, there are certainly some opportunities. For example, the Virtual Reality Medical Center in San Diego specializes in the use of VRET with biofeedback and cognitive behavioral therapy to treat stress, phobias, chronic pain, and anxiety, as well as PTSD.

So how does one start working toward a career in VR or AR for medicine? By taking relevant classes, finding internships or job opportunities, and developing the skills needed for the desired area of future employment.

VRET AT HOME?

While some people find therapy very beneficial, others avoid it for the simple reason that they don't want to talk to a therapist. Some are uncomfortable feeling so emotionally exposed. Others find it hard to keep a scheduled appointment. Some even see talking to a professional as negative. For patients who cannot or do not want to work with a therapist in person but who would still potentially benefit from VRET, there are VR simulations under development that even include a virtual therapist.

A 2017 study in the United Kingdom looked at one hundred adults who had acrophobia—or a fear of heights. Forty-seven of those adults participated in VR sessions with a virtual coach. The virtual coach assessed patients and then invited them to choose the floor of a virtual building and perform such tasks as rescuing a virtual cat from a virtual tree branch. The control group of patients underwent no therapy at all.

The results were promising. In the control group, participants showed very little change in their fear of heights. However, the patients in the group who used coach-led VRET sessions self-reported that their fear of heights decreased significantly, by 68 percent on average. Two weeks after the VRET was completed, the patients were still reporting the decrease in their level of fear.

It's important to know that these patients were assessed by answering questionnaires, which is not a foolproof method of collecting data. Also, one hundred participants make up a relatively small group. Still, the results are positive. There's hope that in the future VRET will be available to more people, perhaps even in the comfort of one's own home.

4 PLANNING FOR A CAREER

For those interested in VR or AR for medicine, there are many opportunities to gain the skills needed to eventually pursue a career in the field. Naturally, the specific steps will depend on the specific part of the field that interests any given person. However, there are a lot of opportunities to gain general exposure to VR, AR, and the field of medicine.

DEGREES FOR DEVELOPERS

For people interested in the software end of VR and AR, a good college degree would be one in computer science. There are specialized computer science degrees at some universities, but a general computer science degree will be available at many colleges.

Opposite: For those wanting a career in the technical end of AR and VR in medicine, it's never too early to start learning how to code or engineer hardware or software.

If a four-year college or university isn't an option right out of high school, students can also start at a community college and gain general-education credits before transferring to a four-year university to complete the degree. Many community colleges also offer two-year degrees called associate's degrees in computer science or a related field.

Among the four-year institutions offering bachelor's degrees in computer science, there are well-known programs at elite universities such as Stanford, Massachusetts Institute of Technology (MIT), and Carnegie Mellon. However, much less expensive and more accessible to many students are countless state universities that also offer degrees in computer science or a related field. There are also countless smaller private universities offering the degree program. While these schools typically come with a high price tag, such universities often offer scholarships. Financial aid and student loans are also options for most universities.

Because VR and AR are fairly new technologies, there aren't a lot of specialized degree programs specifically for them. However, there are a few, and there are certain to be more in the coming years. For example, the University of Advancing Technology in Arizona offers a bachelor's degree in virtual reality. The program focuses on gaming technology because VR and AR are used extensively in gaming. However, the skills are transferable to other fields, such as medicine.

If the highly competitive and elite Stanford University is an option, it is home to the Virtual Human Interaction

Lab. The lab's mission is "to understand the dynamics and implications of interactions among people in immersive virtual reality simulations and other forms of human digital representations in media, communication systems, and games." In other words, they study how people are interacting with virtual worlds and the consequences of those interactions. For those interested in understanding VR's impact on people, this lab is a center of research.

There are also certificate programs for those who pursue different initial degrees, perhaps in medicine or engineering. Cogswell Polytechnical College, located in the Silicon Valley area of California, boasts of being the first college to offer a certificate program in virtual and augmented reality. The classes in the program are designed for students working on another degree in the field or professionals already working in the field. For that reason, the classes are held on evenings and weekends.

For those interested in the hardware development end of VR and AR, a bachelor's degree in computer engineering or electrical engineering is a good starting point. Computer engineering degrees often cover much of the same content as electrical engineering degrees, but with the addition of computer science courses. Students who decide to pursue the more generalized electrical engineering degree are wise to also take classes in computer science or computer programming, since the knowledge is generally a requirement for hardware engineering positions.

While there aren't yet a lot of educational programs that specialize in AR and VR, they are becoming more widespread as the technology becomes more widely available.

CLASSES FOR DEVELOPERS

Long before college, though, there are many classes students can take to begin to prepare themselves for a future in VR and AR. All courses in computer science are a good start, including classes that deal with computer science theory and programming.

Many high schools and even middle schools offer such courses, but students also usually have the option to take classes at the community college level. Community colleges that allow high school students to take classes may offer them online or in person. Often the credits earned are transferrable to the student's high school or to their future university.

For those interested in the artistic side of VR and AR development, art classes are useful. Even when VR

Computer science classes will help you develop a strong foundation for a career in VR or AR.

and AR are being used in a medical setting, there are nearly always art elements involved. For example, VR that generates a representation of a person's internal anatomy requires visual elements to be created and animated. Any classes that offer content in digital or graphic art or 3D modeling will provide an excellent background for students interested in this part of VR and AR development.

In addition, any classes or extracurricular activities that promote collaboration on a team are useful. Technical development is very rarely a solitary activity. Far more often, people are working on their specific piece of a project as part of a much larger team. For that reason, it's extremely important for people interested in the field to demonstrate their ability to collaborate effectively with others. Extracurricular clubs and sports that focus on an activity requiring teamwork are a great way to build up this skill. Being on the school softball team for four years may not seem like it has much to do with VR and AR development or the field of medicine, but it shows that a person can work as part of a team and is motivated to stick with something that is important to them.

RESOURCES FOR DEVELOPERS

It's great to earn a degree in the field or to take classes to prepare for the field, but there are other ways to gain knowledge and experience without setting foot in a classroom. The great thing about the technical development end of VR and AR is that many of the skills can be self-

SUMMER OPPORTUNITIES

For those interested in a career in VR or AR for medicine, not all opportunities center on the traditional school year. There are many chances for skills development during the summer too. Obviously, summer can be a great time for independent work on learning coding and such, but there are more structured ways to gain some experience as well.

There are many camps offering summer programs in VR and AR, though many are focused more on the field of gaming. For those interested in the development end of VR and AR, these can be a great place to learn, though. Knowledge and skills gained in the gaming context can be easily transferred to other fields. These tech camps can be very expensive. However, many offer scholarships. There are also some lower-cost options. In some areas, the Boys & Girls Clubs or Parks and Recreation divisions offer tech camps. Typically, the costs of these are much lower.

Additionally, there is an organization called TryEngineering.org that offers need-based scholarships for students across the United States who are interested in attending engineering camps at the University of California Riverside, Texas A&M University, and Vaughn College of Aeronautics and Technology. The camps aren't specifically focused on VR and AR. However, they focus on engineering challenges that will help students build important problem-solving and teamwork skills.

For those interested in the patient-care side of the industry, there are a great many summer medical programs and internships available. While some of these programs come at a high cost, there are less expensive options as well. Interested students should check the medical facilities in their area to see what's available.

taught. There are plenty of books, internet resources, and online classes for those interested.

There are many excellent web-based resources for learning programming and development. Many offer coding tutorials in common programming languages. For example, Codecademy offers free tutorials in a number of different common programming languages. Learning them will help build a solid foundation for learning more specialized languages. The free tutorials have coding quizzes available, and users can get feedback from professional coaches and advisors. Some of Codecademy's online courses come with a fee, but there are many free ones available as well.

Microsoft Virtual Academy offers free game development training courses online. As mentioned, game development skills are useful to the field of VR and AR for medicine because the technologies needed for both are so similar. If a person can develop VR and AR for a game, they can also develop it for a medical application. A person, however, would need to develop relevant medical knowledge such as anatomy to develop VR and AR for the medical field.

Because Microsoft's HoloLens is showing such promise for medical applications, taking advantage of the free tutorials for VR and AR offered by Microsoft is a wise plan. Those interested in eventually developing VR and AR related to the HoloLens cannot go wrong with learning development techniques directly from the source!

VR and AR applications are generally developed on a game engine. Game engines are used to build gaming environments. Unreal and Unity are popular ones. The Unreal website provides extensive information on developing with the engine. The resources on the website include tutorials, online support, and example scenes and games created with Unreal. Once again, the focus will be on VR and AR for gaming, but the skills are easily transferrable to medical applications. Best of all, this game engine is free.

Similarly, the Unity 3D engine is free. The Unity Technologies website provides opportunities for interested developers to learn. Like the Unreal website, the Unity website offers free tutorials, online projects, and support forums. It also offers fee-based online courses run by Unity Certified Instructors.

Almost any experience in AR or VR can translate to a career in AR or VR for medicine with the appropriate training.

For those interested in the art end of VR and AR development, common 3D art programs include Maya and 3ds Max. Both are fee-based software programs, but both offer free trials. In fact, students can get a free three-year trial of either one. The developer of both software programs, Autodesk, offers online tutorials, downloads, videos, and other resources on its website.

Those who want to experiment with 3D art completely for free can download a free graphics package such as Blender. Blender offers rendering, animation, modeling, and visual effects, just like Maya and 3ds Max. However, the package is entirely free. While future employers may want applicants to know a specific graphics package, such as 3ds Max, typically they are willing to consider applicants who have a good grasp of another similar package. Applicants can usually learn other graphics packages fairly quickly if they already have a good working knowledge of one graphics application.

DEGREE PROGRAMS AND CLASSES FOR MEDICAL PROFESSIONALS

For those more interested in using VR and AR in a medical capacity rather than developing it, the career path looks different. In that case, it's best to pursue medicine generally and take advantage of any training opportunities in using VR in the chosen profession.

For example, a person interested in using VR in the surgical field must go through the typical channels

Learning about AR and VR in medicine doesn't take the place of a traditional medical education; it supplements and enhances it.

to become a surgeon. This involves earning a four-year bachelor's degree and successfully completing four years of medical school. After that, an individual will pursue anywhere from three to ten years of residency and fellowships in surgery. Additionally, an individual must secure the appropriate licenses and certifications along the way. While doing all that, people can choose opportunities that allow them to learn more about how to use VR in the field. For instance, a person can apply to medical schools or residency programs that integrate VR and AR into their coursework.

Similarly, a person interested in becoming a psychologist and practicing VRET must go through the channels to become a psychologist first. A person must earn a four-year bachelor's degree in psychology or a related field, earn a two-year master's degree in psychology or a related field, and then earn a PhD or Psy.D. degree in psychology, which can take an additional two to four years. PhD degrees in psychology are usually for those wishing to work in research. Those interested in working in a clinical setting usually opt for the Psy.D. degree. While doing all that, psychologists can take courses or do clinical rotations or internships that teach them how to use VR in their treatments. The American Psychological Association offers an online list of VR software and training opportunities for psychologists interested in this area of treatment.

Overall, there is a wide range of resources available to individuals interested in this particular career path.

5 NEW OPPORTUNITIES

VR and AR are relatively new fields in general and are quite new in the field of medicine. However, studies on their growth and the general growth in the job market for medicine suggest that there will be many opportunities in the future for those wishing to pursue a career in VR and AR for medicine.

PROJECTED GROWTH

Orbis Research published a market research report in 2017 that suggested the VR market might be greater than $40 billion by the year 2020. This was for the entire VR job market, and VR in medicine is just one part of that. However, it does indicate that VR currently is

Opposite: The field of AR and VR in medicine is growing quickly, and demand for employees will continue to grow as demand for the technology does.

a very profitable field and that it will likely continue to be profitable.

Zion Market Research published a 2017 report predicting that the global AR market would be more than $133 billion by 2021. The report specifically cited a growth rate of more than 85 percent between 2016 and 2021. Once again, this report was for the entire AR market, not just the medical application segment. However, again, it does indicate a promising job market for those interested in pursuing a career in AR development. Clearly there is demand, which means there must be people to fill the jobs in the field.

JOB MARKETS IN VR AND AR

In 2016, the VR market was dominated by a number of large companies, including Sony, Google, and Samsung. Surprisingly, Microsoft ranked relatively low in 2016, but that is likely to change as the HoloLens becomes more widely used.

For those wanting to work specifically on the technical end of VR and AR medical applications, a career path in software is likely to have more job opportunities than a career in hardware. The reason why is that the hardware is largely the same regardless of application. For instance, the same Oculus Rift headsets used for gaming or military training can be used for medical applications. Google Glass devices, wearable glasses with AR capability, are often used in medical applications, but they can also be used in

Google offers many opportunities for people interested in a career in AR and VR.

nonmedical applications. People interested in VR hardware development will certainly find career opportunities—just not necessarily specifically in a medical context.

Software, on the other hand, is industry specific. *Pokémon Go* is strictly a game, for instance. It's not going to be used in the medical field. Likewise, gamers are unlikely

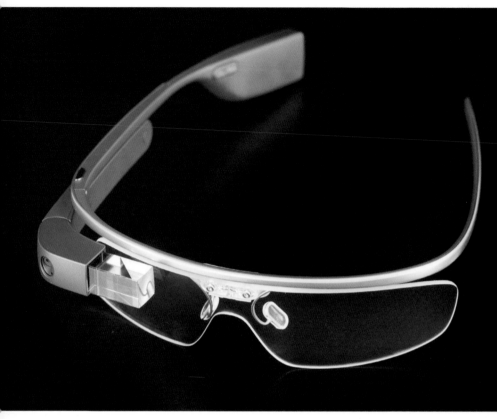

Google Glass was not initially created for surgical purposes; however, some doctors have found the hardware useful.

to want to use Orca Health's AR app that displays 3D anatomical models. The application allows users to view life-size bodies and their anatomies from different angles as though the users were actually walking around a human body. So, for those who wish to combine their passion for medicine with the technical end of VR and AR, a career path in software engineering may be an excellent way to go.

Large Companies Versus Start-Ups

Something to consider as you look forward to future careers is whether you want to work for a large company or a start-up. Large companies typically offer comfortable salaries and strong benefits packages. They also often offer some fun perks. For example, someone interested in a career on Microsoft's HoloLens team is likely to be offered a competitive salary and broad medical benefits. Additionally, Microsoft offers a loan-refinancing program, which can be quite attractive to recent graduates who are starting to pay off six-figure student loans. The tech giant also offers perks such as on-campus shops and services, so employees can take care of shopping, entertainment, and personal care needs during their lunch breaks. To help with travel, Microsoft also offers a shuttle so employees can avoid the notoriously rough commute in the Seattle area, where the company is headquartered. It offers parental leave and a family caregiver plan, which is attractive to those starting a family. The company also often offers to reimburse tuition expenses for classes taken to further one's career. Finally, it has company discounts and a generous charitable giving program.

That all sounds great, right? It probably is. However, those same large companies that offer a lot of fun perks also sometimes expect very long hours from their employees. There are laws in place to protect people from working too long, but it's not unusual for successful companies to expect their employees to go that extra mile. Some people

SEE-THROUGH SURGERY

Israeli company Augmedics is an example of a company producing AR hardware specifically for the medical field. Their xvision headset allows surgeons to see a 3D image of their patients' anatomy. It works with imaging systems to essentially perform see-through surgery. In other words, it equips surgeons with "X-ray vision"—like one might expect in a superhero. This would allow for surgeons to look at the patient as opposed to at a screen or monitor when cutting or drilling into a patient's body. This technology was designed in particular to help with spinal surgeries. In its development phase, it helped surgeons determine the precise location of their tools in order to avoid causing further damage to the patient.

As of 2018, xvision was still in clinical trials, but the results were very promising. Surgeons at Johns Hopkins Hospital placed screws in five cadavers at an accuracy rate of 96.7 percent using the technology. Although developers hoped that the device could be used to increase precision during spinal surgery, other future applications are possible as well.

Company culture is something to consider when thinking about what type of job in the industry to pursue. Will you work alone or in teams?

live for their job and thrive on that kind of fast-paced, demanding environment. However, others prefer to have a work-life balance that leans more toward the "life" end of the spectrum.

Additionally, jobs at major companies can be hard to land. Many people want to work at Microsoft, for example. However, only a small percentage of those individuals end up being offered a position. The demand for Microsoft jobs far outweighs the number of positions available, which is true at most major companies.

Start-up companies can be great places to work for those who can handle a little risk. For instance, UBTECH was a start-up company founded in 2012. In 2018, the company was worth $5 billion.

For those who are a little more inclined to take a risk, a start-up company can be a good option, particularly for those interested in software development. VR and AR hardware are largely manufactured by a few major companies in the industry. However, software can be developed by anyone—even a person coding away in their bedroom on an old laptop. For that reason, start-up software companies are fairly common. It doesn't take much to start a software company if you have a great idea and the skills and talent to pull it off. Hardware typically requires much more of an initial investment because physically creating equipment costs money.

Although this is not true in every case, it can be easier getting a job at a start-up. Not all start-ups will attract the same talent pool as a major company like Microsoft. Start-ups are sometimes willing to hire people with less experience or less education if they see promise in that person's ability to contribute to their team.

There's certainly risk involved in working at a start-up. Start-ups come and start-ups go. Some never end up getting the funding they need to bring their product to the market. Some are beaten to the market by other companies. Some go to market with a product that just doesn't catch on, and the company ends up closing up shop. Depending on the source, statistics show that anywhere between 50 to 90 percent of start-ups fail. Even at the low end of the spectrum of estimates, that means at least one out of every two start-ups fails.

So there's a risk. People have to go into work at a start-up knowing that they might be on the job market again in the near future. However, on the flip side, if the start-up is successful, the employees hired in its early days may end up reaping great rewards. Osso VR is a good example of a successful start-up in medical VR. No doubt cofounders Dr. Justin Barad and psychologist Matt Newport have gained significant prestige as the founders of a successful, award-winning medical VR company and a good deal of wealth from the profits. In 2016, Osso VR was listed as one of the eight VR start-ups to watch at the Emerging Companies Summit.

There is no right or wrong answer to which career path one should take in VR and AR in medicine. In this exciting and rapidly growing field, there will likely be plenty of jobs to come in the future!

GLOSSARY

affective Related to feelings, moods, or attitudes.

augmented reality (AR) This type of computer programming adds computer-generated elements to a user's existing field of vision through devices like a smartphone or smart glasses.

biofeedback A process in which automatic bodily functions are monitored, and the information is used to train a person to acquire control over those functions.

cognitive behavioral therapy A form of therapy in which negative thoughts are challenged in an attempt to alter unwanted behaviors or treat mood disorders.

CT Also called a CAT scan, this is a type of X-ray that produces 360-degree images.

exoskeleton A wearable device, like a bodysuit, that creates physical sensations as part of a virtual reality experience.

haptic force feedback A type of physical response in which force, vibration, or motion is used to virtually create the sense of touch.

hardware The physical equipment that allows for AR and VR experiences, like headsets and controllers.

MRI An acronym for magnetic resonance imaging, a technology that uses high-frequency radio waves and a strong magnetic field to produce images of internal organs.

prototype To create a model of something.

PTSD An acronym for post-traumatic stress disorder, a condition in which mental and emotional distress occur as a result of injury or intense psychological shock.

resident A medical graduate participating in specialized practice under the supervision of an attending physician.

software Programmed instructions that are stored and run inside of hardware to make VR and AR equipment work.

storyboard The creation of a series of drawings that helps designers and engineers plan visuals.

virtual reality (VR) This type of computer programming uses graphics, sounds, and other sensory stimuli to make users feel as if they are inside of a digital environment.

wireframe A skeletal 3D model in which only lines and vertexes are shown.

FURTHER INFORMATION

Books

Allen, John. *Real-World STEM: Improving Virtual Reality*. San Diego: ReferencePoint Press, 2017.

Hulick, Kathryn. *Virtual Reality Developer*. San Diego: ReferencePoint Press, 2017.

Moritz, Jeremy. *Code for Teens: The Awesome Beginner's Guide to Programming*. Herndon, VA: Mascot Books, 2018.

Roland, James. *Careers in Mental Health*. San Diego: ReferencePoint Press, 2017.

Steffens, Bradley. *Careers in Medical Technology*. San Diego: ReferencePoint Press, 2017.

Websites

Careers in Medicine

https://www.aamc.org/cim

This useful website, created by the Association of American Medical Colleges, helps students assess their skills, personality, and future desires to determine which medical specialty may be best suited for them.

Lynda/LinkedIn Learning

https://www.lynda.com

Lynda is a fee-based service that offers more than six hundred courses in software development, more than seven hundred courses in design, and more than seven hundred courses in web development. Interested aspiring developers can sign up for a free month to try out courses.

Microsoft Virtual Academy

https://mva.microsoft.com

This site offers free online training courses for developers. Since Microsoft HoloLens has shown great promise in the medical field, the Microsoft Virtual Academy is a great choice for students interested in relevant technology.

Videos

Using Virtual Reality to Train Physicians for Pediatric Emergencies

https://www.youtube.com/watch?v=LGzzdlAP_S0

This video demonstrates how VR technology can help prepare doctors for certain high-stress situations.

Virtual Reality Is Finding a Place in Health Care

https://www.youtube.com/watch?v=DIvKvkSKeps

This video demonstrates how VR can be used to serve surgical patients, lessening their anxiety levels by providing a virtual experience of their hospital stays.

SELECTED BIBLIOGRAPHY

"Augmented Reality (AR) Market (Sensor, Display, and Software) for Aerospace & Defense, Industrial, Consumer, Commercial, E-commerce, Retail and Other Applications: Global Industry Perspective, Comprehensive Analysis, Size, Share, Growth, Segment, Trends, and Forecast, 2015–2021." Zion Market Research, November 23, 2016. https://www.zionmarketresearch.com/report/augmented-reality-market.

"Computer Programmers." Bureau of Labor Statistics: Occupational Outlook Handbook. Accessed December 1, 2018. https://www.bls.gov/ooh/computer-and-information-technology/computer-programmers.htm#tab-5.

Condliffe, Jamie. "AR Is Making Its Way into the OR." *MIT Technology Review*, May 11, 2017. https://www.technologyreview.com/s/607852/ar-is-making-its-way-into-the-or.

Davis, Nicola. "Automated Virtual Reality Therapy Helps People Overcome Phobia of Heights." *Guardian*, July 11, 2018. https://www.theguardian.com/science/2018/jul/11/automated-virtual-reality-therapy-helps-people-overcome-phobia-of-heights.

———. "Cutting-Edge Theatre: World's First Virtual Reality Operation Goes Live." *Guardian*, April 14, 2016. https://www.theguardian.com/ technology/2016/apr/14/cutting-edge-theatre-worlds-first-virtual-reality-operation-goes-live.

Fink, Charlie. "How VR Saves Lives in the OR." *Forbes*, September 28, 2017. https://www.forbes.com/sites/ charliefink/2017/09/28/how-vr-saves-lives-in-the-or/#73e82d4e3099.

"Global Virtual Reality Market (Hardware and Software) and Forecast to 2020." Orbis Research, February 6, 2017. http://www.orbisresearch.com/ reports/index/global-virtual-reality-market-hardware-and-software-and-forecast-to-2020.

Lake, James. "Virtual Reality Graded Exposure Therapy (VRGET)." *Psychology Today*, November 6, 2017. https://www.psychologytoday.com/us/blog/ integrative-mental-health-care/201711/virtual-reality-graded-exposure-therapy-vrget.

LaMotte, Sandee. "The Very Real Health Dangers of Virtual Reality." CNN, December 13, 2017. https://www.cnn.com/2017/12/13/health/virtual-reality-vr-dangers-safety/index.html.

Laurent, Olivier. "This Doctor Used Snapchat's Spectacles to Record a Surgery." *Time*, December 12, 2016. http://time.com/4597434/snapchat-spectacles-snap-surgery.

Li, Angela, Zorash Montaño, Vincent J. Chen, and Jeffrey I. Gold. "Virtual Reality and Pain Management: Current Trends and Future Directions." *Pain Management* 1, no. 2 (March 2011): 147–157. doi: 10.2217/pmt.10.15.

"Mission." Virtual Human Interaction Lab. Accessed December 1, 2018. https://vhil.stanford.edu/mission.

"Psychologists." Bureau of Labor Statistics: Occupational Outlook Handbook. Accessed December 1, 2018. https://www.bls.gov/ooh/life-physical-and-social-science/psychologists.htm.

Reynolds, Matt. "Augmented Reality Goggles Give Surgeons X-ray Vision." *New Scientist*, May 11, 2017. https://www.newscientist.com/article/2130678-augmented-reality-goggles-give-surgeons-x-ray-vision.

Schmidt, Elaine. "Fighting Memory Loss with Virtual Reality." University of California News, August 31, 2017. https://www.universityofcalifornia.edu/news/fighting-memory-loss-virtual-reality.

"Software Developers." Bureau of Labor Statistics: Occupational Outlook Handbook. Accessed December 1, 2018. https://www.bls.gov/ooh/computer-and-information-technology/software-developers.htm#tab-1.

INDEX

ABOUT THE AUTHOR

Cathleen Small is the author of more than sixty books for students in middle school and high school. Before making the switch to writing, Small was an editor for a technical publisher for nearly twenty years, where she edited hundreds of books on game development, programming, applications, and more. When she's not writing, Small enjoys traveling and spending time with her family in the San Francisco Bay Area.